The Death of My Uterus
and Other Humorous Events

A Collection of Stories, Poems, and Limericks
about the Indignities of Cancer

D1416010

by Carrie A. Horwitch
illustrations by Kristen Bannister

This book is dedicated to my family and friends
for sharing this experience and
bringing joy and love into my life.

Contents

The Death of My Uterus

Once upon a time not so long ago
Lived a girl always on the go
She lived life to the fullest
Never one to be dullest
'Til the death of her uterus

Now the story began in the fall
She started swelling up like a ball
It was down in her belly
And much firmer than jelly
A hint to the death of her uterus

Next step was the abdominal ultrasound
Where a large pelvic mass was to be found
To the surgeon she went
To find out what it meant
Moving closer to the death of her uterus

He thought the mass might be benign
As there was no other ominous sign
But surgery was needed
Advice soon to be heeded
Not expecting the death of her uterus

After surgery I heard the bad news
And all that I came to lose
He said, "So sorry, my dear
You had cancer right here"
And it was the death of my uterus

In addition to all the other fuss
Came info far more momentous
For unlike Madame Bovary's
I had lost both my ovaries
Another plus to the death of my uterus

Now children I'd been unable to bear
Previously I thought I didn't care
But I still held out hope
Making it easier to cope
The final step was the death of my uterus

This personal story could end right here
But we'd lose something that is quite dear
Life holds so much more
When we open a new door
The end is not the death of my uterus

So now I say don't wallow in sorrow
For there is a chance at tomorrow
I wake up and pray
To smile each day
I'm alive since the death of my uterus

My Story

"They had to take everything."
Those were the five words that changed my life in an instant.

I was coming out of my anesthetic fog after surgery for what we all hoped was a benign mass. Instead, those five words meant I had ovarian cancer. I was not happy about this. I was now marked for life, not from the scars of the surgery, but from the diagnosis of being a cancer patient. As I embarked on the Kubler-Ross's five stages of grieving: denial, anger, bargaining, depression, and acceptance, I wrote to help explain and control my situation. Light, warmth, hope, and healing were my buzz words. Until I discovered a new one—laughter.

This book is about hope, laughter, and smiling in the face of adversity. This book is about transitioning through a strenuous time and getting to the other side with my integrity and humor intact.

My goal for writing this book is to bring hope and inspiration to others. I believe we must laugh in the face of fearful events. Allow ourselves to feel normal when life is not "normal," and to feel a sense of control, where mostly we have none. Give this book to anyone who wants a good laugh or a smile.

The story actually started four weeks earlier when I noted some vague swelling in my lower abdomen. It was strange as I only noted this at night just as I was falling asleep. For a couple of nights, I thought I might be dreaming it. However, by the third night I knew something was wrong. There was no pain, no other symptoms, but I hastened to my doctor, who ordered an ultrasound. The ultrasound confirmed that the endometrioma (that I have had for years) was enlarged from previous exams.

After surgery and the sentence that changed everything, I was trying to process that information, trying not to vomit from the narcotics they gave me at surgery and trying not to show my fear at the diagnosis.

I had gone from a healthy person to a "sick" one, and I was pissed to be labeled that way. This started my fight for how I was going to deal with this disease and gain back some control over it.

It was during the first several days of recovery that I had an event that changed how I was going to manage my diagnosis. Friends came over to visit and stayed for dinner. During the dinner, I started getting some uncomfortable pain (like passing gas) in my abdomen. I had been eating and passing gas since I left the hospital (they won't let you leave unless you can show this) but I had not had a bowel movement yet. That was going to change this evening—but it was not a pleasant experience.

I excused myself and made my way to the bathroom. I felt better bending over in the fetal position but nothing happened except the gas seemed to pass…for the moment. I rejoined everyone at the table, but a few minutes later the same pain happened again. This happened two of three more times, and by then I just stayed in the bathroom waiting. I was lying on the bathroom floor in a fetal position with my face against the cool tile. At some point, our friends left. Who can blame them? No one wants to be around for the first extrusion of stool.

My husband stuck his head in the door to see if I was alright. I remember answering him, "If this doesn't get any better, just shoot me now." He was not amused, but I had found a tool to deal with my illness…sarcasm and humor. This event also prompted my limerick writing, one that would continue to sustain me and give me moments of belly laughter at the absurdness of what was happening.

Here's the limerick that started it all off…

Post-Surgical Blues

The doctor's waiting for something to pass
In the form of a little bowel gas
Easy for him to say
But I say, "Oy Vey!"
'Cause it feels like sharp glass through my ass

As a physician, I am well aware that health is not just confined to the physical but also encompasses our emotional and spiritual well-being. I was leaving the physical part (the surgery, the chemo, etc.) to the doctors taking care of me. I was the only one who could be in charge of my emotional and spiritual wellness. I exercised every day no matter how I felt, I started to eat better (cutting out sugar and caffeine), I wrote in a journal about the experience, and I put my name on the get well lists at my synagogue (and asked others to place my name on their lists as well).

I got lots of advice from friends and family about what books to read, what to do, and what organizations to look into. I looked at several books to find inspiration, but mostly what I read was maudlin and depressing. I needed to do this my way.

My First Visit for Chemotherapy

My husband and I entered the chemotherapy clinic and waited while the receptionist ended her phone call. She looked up from her computer and asked me what I was there for. An odd question given that this was the chemotherapy clinic. So I answered, "I'm here to get toxic chemicals poured into my body." She gave me a blank stare as if she either didn't hear my answer or wasn't sure I would be so irreverent about something so serious. Hmm, I thought they can use a serious dose of laughter in this place.

Chemotherapy and its subsequent side effects inspired several limericks. I sent out new limericks to my friends and family with each chemotherapy treatment. It helped them understand what was happening, gave them a laugh, and allowed them to join in the fun of writing.

The Laughter Club

Limerick writing was just the beginning in my quest for healing through humor. The next step was inspired by a flyer on the wall of my doctor's office, advertising a laughter club. I was intrigued and made a point to go to the next one being offered.

I entered the room hesitantly. The room was small, maybe twelve feet by twelve feet, and painted a uniform grayish white, typical for a hospital corridor. The fluorescent lights overhead were bright and made everyone's skin look a little yellow.

There were already a few people sitting around the table. Some clearly had cancer given their bald heads and thinning cheeks. Some were connected to their chemo by IV tubing, and others were support people. I was alone and thankful I didn't recognize anyone in the group. The room became crowded. There were at least twenty people taking every seat around the table.

The laughter club leader came in wearing a jester's hat and a red nose, ready to get us started. She gave a brief overview of what a laughter club was and how she got started. We warmed up our bodies with a series of deep breathing exercises and then followed with the laughter warm up of "Ho Ho Ha Ha Ha".

Soon we were all laughing and looking incredibly silly as she led us through one laugh exercise after another: The ski jump, the penguin walk, the greeting laughs, and many others. For the next forty minutes, we laughed until our sides hurt and tears rolled down our cheeks. It was fantastic, and I felt so energized and happy. I knew I had found my inspiration to get through the chemo treatments and whatever else life threw in my way.

Laughter really helps!

Laughing My Way Through Chemo

I put laughter to the acid test during my chemo treatments. For an hour before the actual chemotherapy started came all the pre-medications to reduce the risk of a reaction to the chemo. There was the obligatory anti-nausea medication followed by steroids and an antihistamine to reduce any allergic reaction to the chemo. By the time this was all done, I was not sure whether I should walk a mile or go to sleep, since the medications have opposite effects. It also made reading almost impossible as my eyes wanted to close one minute and snap wide open the next.

Now for the toxic chemicals—otherwise known as chemotherapy. You know when it arrives because the nurses gown, glove, and mask so as not to touch any part of the chemotherapy itself. If anyone doubts that chemo is toxic, you have only to look at the precautions that are taken by the nurses.

Once the chemo started and no immediate reaction ensued, the nurse left to care for other patients. It was boring sitting there. I tried to sleep but was not able to. I walked around a little, dragging the IV pole with me. I decided to apply what I had learned at the laughter club. I started with the simple laughs, "Hee, Hee, Ha, Ha, Ho, Ho". Then I went on to some others I had learned like "Achy back, Lions laugh". Bewildered, the nurse poked her head around the curtain to see what was happening and even joined in the fun. Here was one way to make the minutes and hours go faster and funnier. Friends would come by to visit, and I would have them do the laughs with me.

Spreading the Joy

Even after the seven months of surgery, chemotherapy, and recovery, I kept using the laughter in new and useful ways. I started researching and reading about laughter and its various health benefits, including improving energy, reducing stress hormones, improving blood vessel flow and lung function, burning calories, and more. The more I read and studied the more I realized I was going to make this part of my well-being activity and teach it to others. I decided to get certified as a "Laughter Leader". I started giving lectures at work and at local and national meetings about the benefits of laughter. I even started to judiciously teach some exercises to select patients I thought would benefit from this technique.

Bringing laughter to others has been so rewarding that I wanted to find a way to spread it more widely, and so I set out to publish this book of limericks in hopes of bringing a little lightness, companionship, and hope to others undergoing the strange and peculiar indignities of cancer treatment.

Chapter 1

Under the Knife

Many people offered words of advice before I went under the knife (well-meaning, I'm sure, but not all of them were taken well), including one friend who wondered whether my last will and testament was in order. I thought that an odd and somewhat disturbing comment before I embarked on a major surgery.

Night Before Surgery

'Twas the night before surgery
And we're in our house
I was sitting there quietly
Just me and my spouse

All of a sudden there was
A knock on the door
Two friends came over
To show support and more

The visit was pleasant
Up to the moment
When my friend said something
Not sure what it meant

Her words hit me hard
And sent a chill up my spine
For she asked me point-blank
If I had a will, that was mine

My husband heard this too
And took immediate action
When he looked at my face
And saw my shocked reaction

He said, "Now's the time
For you two to leave
Thank you for coming
On this surgery eve"

After they left
And we were alone
We had to laugh
In face of that serious tone

The lesson in this poem
To all those who visit
Be careful what you say
Or your friends may regret it

One thing people will note about surgical suites is how cold they are. I honestly don't know why these areas are so cold. Maybe, it has to do with the machinery or maybe it's so the surgeons aren't sweating too much when they're working. I doubt it has any effect on bacteria, but the areas are freezing. It used to be that a patient was be piled up with blankets heated in a special oven, which was very nice. Now there are devices that blow warm air through a sterile drape to keep you warm. One device company (and there are several) calls it a Bair Hugger. This is fabulous, no more goose bumps and shivering.

Bair Hug

Surgery suites are kept cold as ice
To keep bacteria from spreading like lice
So now the new norm
To keep the patient warm
Is the great Bair Hugger device

Chapter 1 **Under the Knife**

Some doctors can say the wrong thing
Like think of cancer as a blessing
Are they unaware?
Or do they not care?
That this diagnosis is mostly distressing

There are those who say cancer's a blessing
Seems to me it's a time for confessing
I'd rather receive
A cancer reprieve
Believe me as I'm professing my stressing

Chapter 2

Body Functions

Let's be honest—we've all had the occasional issue with bowel dysfunction (perhaps along with other body irregularities). It's neither pleasant nor really funny. But I have to say that this one area lent itself to some of the more visual limericks than any other aspect of this unwanted adventure in my life.

Body Functions

Every day with my morning ablution
I look for a stool contribution
If one is not had
It's exceedingly bad
And I pray for a prompt resolution

There is no more distressing sensation
Than that of severe constipation
Though this movement of bowel
May be painful or foul
Its passage is met with jubilation

It is my sincerest belief
That one must have rapid relief
Ignore this advice
You'll pay a big price
And give you nothing but grief

Some women are seen as classy
While others are short and sassy
But me, I'm unique
Though I'm not very chic
'Cause I sure am one gassy lassie

Chapter 3
Hair Today, Gone Tomorrow

The plethora of side effects and symptoms is quite extensive. I remember one oncologist, when I asked him about hair loss (something that was very concerning for me since it is the most obvious sign you have cancer), he merely patted his bald head and said, "At least yours will grow back." I was absolutely stunned that a physician would say something so callous. I had long hair and considered it one of my best features. The loss of hair was something I knew was inevitable but I also didn't want it to happen. Who says there's logic when facing an unpleasant future event! However, I did my best to rally with the times and the limericks flowed.

Hair Today, Gone Tomorrow

The male doctor said I should be glad
My hair loss is not really so bad
"At least yours will grow back
Unlike me, which I lack"
His callous comment made me boiling mad

Chapter 3 **Hair Today, Gone Tomorrow**

There once was a girl named Carrie
Who was known to be quite hairy
But early one dawn
Her hair was all gone
Now she looks more like bald Larry

Michael got up one day and said,
"There is hair all over the bed
I'm in a bit of a fog
'Cause we don't have a dog"
Then he spied his wife's naked head

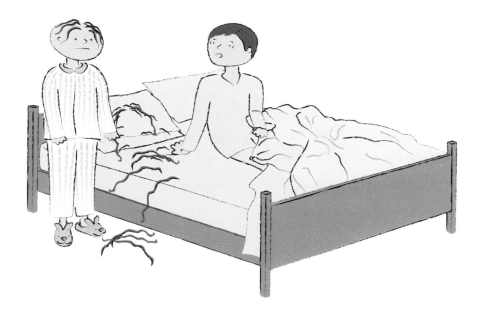

Chapter 3 **Hair Today, Gone Tomorrow**

My friends said it would really be boss
To get a wig for the expected hair loss
I had an expensive one made
For which I so dearly paid
But it looked as foreign as a head full of moss

The hair loss was really complete
From my head on down to my feet
Chemo left not a hair
Which worked better than Nair
It will sure be a treat when they replete

Chapter 3 **Hair Today, Gone Tomorrow**

If you think hair loss causes concern, regrowth of hair has its own interesting challenges. My hair started growing back a little at a time. Luckily the eyelashes and brows came back first, allowing my face to look normal again. Then the hair on my head grew back VERY slowly and grey. "Oh no" was my first thought, to be grey before the age of fifty. Luckily, the color faded and my hair came back several shades darker than before and curly. I had never had curly hair, and it was fun. When people asked me about my curls, I said, "I just had one of the most expensive perms in the world."

Hair Again

My hair has now started to grow
Although it is going too slow
There's a tuft here and there
And it's grey everywhere
Just like the glow of cold snow

Since chemo's done my doc said, "See ya"
Things will improve I guarantee ya
The hair's growing back
But I gasp and say, "Aack"
Now my head looks like a ch-ch-chia

Chapter 3 **Hair Today, Gone Tomorrow**

My new hair growth is really hip
At least that's what others all quip
It came back brown and grey
In three months and a day
But to me looks like a dingy Q-tip

Chapter 4

Better Living
Through Chemicals

Hair loss is only one of a multitude of side effects chemo can give you. There is the bone marrow suppression (the part of the body that makes all your blood cells red, white, and platelet), nausea, numbness, mood changes, abnormal taste, more bowel issues, fatigue, the annoyance of taking pills, and feelings of isolation. I wrote limericks about all of these. It helped to laugh and joke about what really was not very funny and quite serious.

Better Living Through Chemicals

Some say getting cancer isn't so bad
Clearly it's something they never had
'Tween the labs and the drugs
One feels like a slug-bug
Making me feel both sad and mad

Don't fool yourself into a trap
When they say chemo is a snap
It might be well-meaning
But it's honestly dreaming
That saying is sure full of crap

I have trouble taking one pill
While others can take them at will
With a bit of good luck
Then I won't upchuck
But the thrill of the drill is still nil

Chapter 4 **Better Living Through Chemicals**

My white count is down in the dumps
Need to lay low for now 'til it jumps
For I'm prone to disease
From the littlest sneeze
I'll look as if I just got the mumps

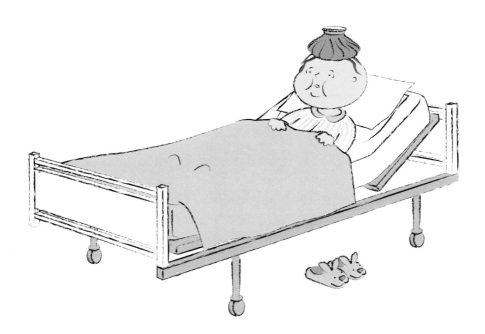

There once was a girl from Bohemia
Whose treatment caused her anemia
Her bone marrow failed
And that's why she paled
'Course there was also severe neutropenia

My neutrophils got so low I freaked out
And put my chemo regimen in some doubt
My doc said, "Not to worry
It will come up in a hurry
But we can now reduce the amount"

My platelet count really went down
Caused me to delay chemo and frown
It took quite some time
But they eventually did climb
So now can go back to downtown

Nausea is not very funny
It's focused right down in the tummy
The foods and the smell
Make me feel crappy as hell
And up comes that tea with the honey

There once was a young girl from Lubbock
Whose chemo made her sick to her stomach
The smell of the food
Made her feel not so good
And ran to the loo in one mach

A few days after the chemo settles
Food and water taste like heavy metals
No need to make haste
'Cause cooking's a waste
When it tastes like my bicycle pedals

Chapter 4 **Better Living Through Chemicals**

Post-chemo fatigue is the pits
It surprises you when it hits
Just like a tsunami
On the Isle of Pastrami
As quick as the blitz hits then it quits

Just when things were going so well
My right leg started to swell
I'm thankful a lot
There wasn't a clot
But I dwell on the swell that won't quell

A new chemo bonus, "Oh brother"
One leg's now bigger than the other
Lymphedema's the name
Cancer's to blame
It's always one thing or another

Now the chemo's affected my nerves
A new side effect I observe
It hits like a jolt
Of a hundred watt volt
Another complication that I don't deserve

I thought I was now in the clear
But what happened next justified fear
My fingers are numb
It goes and then comes
A consequence of the chemo last year

My joints are now achy and sore
They hurt all the way down to the core
It's not cancer or arthritis
Maybe a chemo incidentalitis
But this pain I don't want anymore

About health I have some illusions
But I've come to some new conclusions
Your vision starts fading
As the joints keep degrading
These illusions are more like delusions

I was feeling depressed and disdained
In loneliness I was enmeshed and remained
My counts hit the ground
And the flu was around
But the limericks kept me quite entertained

Chapter 5
After All That...Menopause!

Most women will go through menopause. It's a natural phenomenon of aging. To be thrown into surgical menopause with no warning or no gradual ramp up was a shock. Thankfully it was winter so being warm was less onerous than it could have been, but the experience was in a word…annoying. To describe this to others I use the analogy of internal combustion bubbling up in the body for several minutes and then disappearing just as quickly…until the next time.

After All That...Menopause!

Every hour I get sweaty and hot
'Cause of hormones that I haven't got
They say that one day
These will just go away
But I thought not to get caught in this spot

So now I have blasted hot flashes
From my toes up to my eyelashes
I just want to weep
They're disrupting my sleep
I toss the blankets away with the thrashes

I'm tired and not getting sleep
Even while trying to count sheep
It's the blasted hot flashes
Feeling like I've got rashes
Like laying in a deep heap of... "Bleep!"

Hot flashes are certainly the pits
Means tossing and turning in fits
I have internal heat
From my head to my feet
And wreaks havoc on my flagging wits

There should really be several laws
Against immediate surgical menopause
With all estrogen gone
I wake up now each dawn
When internal combustion comes on without cause

Chapter 6

Recovery

RECOVERY: a wonderful word—the end of chemo and the return to what I hoped to be my previous state of good health. It too was a process and one that did not go as fast as I wanted. I looked to find improvement each day—no matter how small.

I used laughter every day, either by myself or with friends and when writing limericks. On walks, I would just start laughing (sometimes causing my hubby to run ahead of me and then I would chase him and we would both be holding our sides in laughter). It was amazing to see how people watching us would smile and laugh as well. Laughter truly is contagious.

Recovery

Up to now my activities were suspended
Being careful to stay well, I depended
Now the sun has come out
And I wander about
As my last round of chemo has ended

Every day I get better and stronger
Soon my isolation will be no longer
To work I will go
And get on with the flow
Which is better than feeling humonger

Through winter I was in hibernation
Since chemo ended I have liberation
I go here and there
With people everywhere
Recreation now brings new revelation

My strength returns in bits and droves
Almost as fast as my hair grows
I still need to rest
To be at my best
How long it will take, only God knows

The support I've received is astounding
From family and friends it's abounding
From the heavens above
I've been given such love
Hope resounds in me and my surroundings

I now want to say on my behalf
I look for any occasion to laugh
It improves my mood
As it's not good to brood
And I don't care who thinks that I'm daft

Having had cancer you learn a thing or two
Like how to avoid singing the blues
When the chemo's all through
You sing a big whoop-de doo
And figure out what the hell next to do

To look out for my own behalf
I kept up my ability to laugh
It wasn't so easy
When I felt queasy
'Cause at times I made a big gaffe

There are things that I wouldn't dare
Like go a day without offering a prayer
For continued good health
Which I prize above wealth
And share my prayer for those who need care

Laughter is what I did to cope
The alternative was to sit and mope
I looked quite silly
To ha ha willy nilly
But to do so gave me greater hope

Chapter 7

I Get by with a Little Help from My Friends

Once I started writing the limericks, my friends and family got in the groove of writing them as well. They kept asking what they could do to help. I told them I wanted stories, and I wanted them to keep me smiling and laughing. Their limericks and poems made a big difference. Some were in support of my trials and tribulations and others were for their own issues they were facing.

Limericks from Others

Ode to a Liberal
A gal from Seattle did write
A limerick both funny and bright
She's smart and she's able
And one you can't label
Except being "left," she's so right

Sorry your white count is low
Hope soon you'll be rid of this foe
Glad you are keeping everything light
Because I know your future is bright

There once was a girl named Wendy
Who used to be quite bendy
She got the MS
Which gave her distress
But now, she's again on the mendy

My beautiful Carrie has gotten
Some news that her cells hit rock bottom
After a whirlwind of questions
And some other suggestions
Three week treatments remain the best choice

There once was a girl from Seattle
Who has talismans for health who can rattle
She sent some to Ron
For what he's undergone
And if anything will make him better that'll

There once was a lass name of Carrie
Who traveled to us via ferry
She was flat on her ass
Trying to pass gas
Which would work if she'd mix meat with dairy

You're halfway through chemo by now
I know you can do it (and how!)
The secret's not tricky
When you start feeling icky
Eat Vitamin CH and…Wow!

Cancer brings you into contact with many different people who share their stories of challenging situations. Limericks are so flexible they can be used to bring humor (sarcastic, though it is) to others who are facing their own challenges. These are limericks I wrote for others who I was fortunate to encounter on my journey.

Limericks to Others

There is a girl named Astrid Pujari
Who takes her clients on a mind-body safari
They close their eyes
And await their surprise
To go from Bali to the vast Kalahari

I have heard a suspicious rumor
That you have an obnoxious tumor
That news sure does suck
But there is some good luck
It should not affect your witty humor

I met a gent with cancer of his bladder
He took life head on and didn't seem to matter
I asked, "How could this be?
Cancer's bad, don't you see?"
He smiled and said, "Better to be happy not sadder"

There is a young man named Ron
Whose prostate is now all gone
He makes a wish
That it's easy to pish
On his way to use the john

Chapter 7 **I Get by with a Little Help from My Friends**

When she was diagnosed with a polyp
The treatment gave her quite a wallop
A real pain in the ass
Was caused by this mass
This polyp was much more than a dollop

Allan's a man who has been quite mellow
Unexpectedly one day he turned bright yellow
Pancreatic cancer was found
Turned his world all around
"Hell, no, I won't go," this fellow now bellows

I acquired a side effect most dreaded
My esophagus feels like it's shredded
Whenever I swallow
The pain then does follow
So to Mylanta I'm truly indebted

There is a young gent named Paul
Who went skiing and took quite a fall
He broke some rib bones
Causing gasps, moans, and groans
Which made him stall to a crawl after all

There is a young man named Henry
Who agrees to send out this plea,
"Despite the lost hair
I really do care
That you see I'm free to be me"

Heard your hip was being a pain
Making walking difficult to maintain
But now it's replaced
You'll recover post-haste
To dance without strain once again

I have a wonderful friend Jill
Who knows cancer can be a real pill
First it was the breasts
Then went on to bone mets
But she still gets life's fill with strong will

I know a young man whose name is Corey
Whose issue deals with his guts, not his glory
He seemed very pissed
When told he has GIST
He will have a good "clear" end to this story

Acknowledgements

This book would not have been possible without the hard work and dedication of my publishing consultant, Ensley Eikenburg. Her guidance, perseverance, encouragement, and enthusiasm for this project made this book a reality. She also laughed at my many jokes and limericks, which reaffirmed our conviction that this book is important to share with others.

A thank you also needs to go to our mutual friend, Sally Kassab. It was serendipity that both Ensley and I visited Sally at the same time.

To Kristen Bannister for her fabulous illustrations that bring the limericks to life.

To the World Laughter Tour, which trained me to be a laughter leader that led to my incorporating laughter into my personal wellness program and teach it to others.

To my doctors, nurses, and health care team members, who saved my life, helped me navigate this process, and gave me hope.

To my husband, Michael, who kept me walking daily, plotted out my blood counts on spread sheets, and supported me in so many wonderful and loving ways throughout this journey.

To my family and friends, who always support me in pursuit of my dreams and who gave unconditional love, prayers, and laughter.

About the Author

Carrie A. Horwitch is an internal medicine physician. She is dedicated to working with patients throughout their lives. She has special expertise in taking care of patients with HIV. She has traveled to several African countries as part of a team of educators to train health care workers in the care of HIV patients in resource limited settings. She also trains residents in Internal Medicine. Dr. Horwitch received her certificate as a laughter leader from World Laughter Tour. She has given dozens of lectures at local and national conferences on the benefits of laughter for health and wellness. This is her first book.